Preschool: At What Cost?

Susan K. Stewart

Preschool: At What Cost?
Published by Practical Inspirations
P. O. Box 561
Luling, TX 78648
www.practicalinspirations.com

ISBN 978-069221385-8
Library of Congress Control Number

Although every effort has been made to ensure the accuracy and appropriateness of the Internet sites and links mentioned in this book, the author and publisher have no control over and assume no liability for the material available on these websites or other links they are connected to.

Cover Photo:

Cover Design: Marty Molina
GraphicType
Brea, CA

Printed in the United States of America

Contents

Acknowledgments

While a writer may hunch over the keyboard alone, it is not solitary work. In fact I say writing a book requires a team, and I had one of the best.

Author Cecil Murphey invests his time to help and mentor other writers. I've been privileged to be one of them. Cec has not only taught me important details of writing, he has also been an encourager.

No written piece is perfect. And no writer lets an article or book see the light of day without someone else finding the mistakes first. My outstanding editors, Bethany Bennett, Karen Koch, and Peggy Taylor, withstood the multiple versions as they pointed out all of my writing sins. Their eagle eyes have made this publication possible.

Sometimes a writer has a book in mind, but a little extra push from the outside is needed. My dear friend Susan Beatty was my pusher. Not only did she help me hone the idea, Susan also knew just the right times to nudge me along to get it done.

I've also had a team member who is behind the scenes, my life partner Bob. He has been my supporter, sounding board, and cheerleader. Like many spouses of writers, he has endured while I have spent more time with my computer than with him. That is just one small reason why I love him.

I thank each member of my team for making this book a reality.

Introduction

"My child will be two next month, what curriculum should I buy?" Some of you maybe thinking, "Well, yeah, I have the same question." Some of you may be chuckling, while others are shaking their heads, thinking, "No, no! Don't do it." For parents who have decided to teach their preschoolers at home, asking curriculum to use is more common than asking, "What about socialization?"

It hasn't been long ago that attending an out-of-home preschool was uncommon, and in many cases, it was optional. If a child attended, it was a couple days a week of short intervals of social and play activities for three- and four-year-olds, or an all-day program that provided child care for working parents. Making the leap to homeschooling your preschooler with these circumstances is not as wide a chasm as making the leap if you doubt your ability to parent your young children.

Doubting your ability to parent your young children is exactly the impact the widely publicized campaign for Universal Preschool has achieved since the mid-1990s. Preschool has evolved from a place of play and playmates to formal, sit-at-the-desk academics. Being ready to learn no longer means having a good breakfast. It means entering kindergarten prepared with early math skills, writing skills, and pre-reading skills, if the child is not already reading.

Headlines abound stating children are so severely disadvantaged by not attending to preschool they will become dropout criminals. Articles quote studies, statistics, and experts to prove the case for early childhood education.

Valerie wrote on a preschool email list

A long-recurring thought of mine is IF programs have been in place for so long, why do we not see the academic progress we have been looking for, and if we did see it, what would it look like?

She goes on with

Head Start began in 1965, and if children have benefited from programs for over forty years, why are we not seeing parents who benefited raising better children? When do the results kick in? Are the wrong things being taught?

If there is no result in a subsequent generation of people who were provided a program, then what is the point?

Let Valerie's questions sink in for a moment. What are the answers to her questions? Have there really been the well-publicized gains for children and our society?

When parents began asking me what curriculum they should buy for their almost two-year-old, I began to ask why. From parents I learned that even parents who intended to homeschool were considering out-of-home preschool so their little one would get a good foundation for their education. Parents worry they will somehow ruin their child's future by not having early academics, either out-of-home or in-home.

Parent anxiety has increased to the point some have begun to believe if academics aren't started before potty training, their child won't have a successful future. The push for academics has left important aspects of child development behind, including social development.

This anxiety concerned me enough to begin reading the articles and studies. My children had grown to productive adults without preschool. Had life in the United States changed so much in twenty-five years?

What I found was when California attempted to mandate Universal Preschool the push for earlier and earlier school attendance began. I also found that the statistics and reports most often quoted were not the whole story. Not published are a host of reports and studies that don't support out-of-home preschool programs for young children.

In fact, I found literature that explains why early academics, *even at home*, are not particularly beneficial to any preschool-aged child. I've learned by experience and research that play, character training, and learning appropriate social skills can be a better foundation for later success. I wrote this book to share what I discovered with you.

Before buying workbooks, sitting down with the Leapster®, or signing up for the latest preschool activity class, consider if a different approach might be best for your child. Is it possible that uninterrupted, unstructured play may teach more than the adult-created academic activities?

As you consider the best way to prepare your preschool-aged child for future education think about what is important for your child. It's not always what the so-called experts claim. Remember, God has given you the authority to make that decision.

1

History of Preschool

"Does she go to preschool?" the nurse asked about our three-year-old granddaughter. When our reply was no, she looked as though she didn't know how to respond. Bob explained, as long as our granddaughter was living with us, she wouldn't be going to school. That only brought more blank stares.

Until recently preschool was an uncommon option. If a child attended one, it was a couple days a week of short intervals of social and play activities for three- and four-year-olds, or all-day programs that provided child care for working parents.

In the 1990s, the mantra became "all children enter kindergarten ready to learn," setting the stage for the Universal Preschool movement early in the 21st century. Only since California attempted to mandate Universal Preschool did this early education option become thought of as a requirement.

Preschool has evolved from a place of play and friends to formal, sit-at-the-desk academics. Being ready to learn no longer means having a good breakfast. It means entering kindergarten prepared with early math skills, writing skills, and pre-reading skills, if not already reading.

Until the beginning of the twentieth century, no one thought of sending children under the age of five or six away from the loving environment of their home. In some cases, it wasn't mandatory for children to leave home for school until the age of eight. The notion of sending young children away from home for learning is relatively new. So, too, is the idea that toddlers and preschoolers need formal academics.

A Place to Play

Kindergartens began as a place to play. Friedrich Froebel, a German naturalist and philosopher, is credited with starting the first kindergartens—children's garden—in 1837. He named his kindergarten the Play and Activity Center. Designed for children aged four and five years, Froebel's kindergarten's primary focus was on play. Unlike the traditional view of the time, which said play was unworthy and held no value, Froebel believed play provided an environment for children to develop.

Although Froebel's intent was for parents to use his method at home, the royalty wanted their children to attend these schools. It is recorded that Froebel's love for nature and strong Christian faith were central to his educational thinking. [1]

In its beginning, early childhood education wasn't academic. It was social and spiritual. German immigrants, fleeing the failed Prussian revolution, brought kindergarten to the United States. Margarethe Meyer Schurz came to America by way of England, bringing with her Froebel's ideas, which she used with her young daughter Agathe.

The Schurzs settled in Watertown, Wisconsin, where Margarethe gathered other young children to play with her daughter. Margarethe continued to use the informal play activities of Froebel. Others in Watertown were impressed with the achievements of these young children, and eventually Margarethe opened the first American kindergarten in 1855.

Elizabeth Peabody, a nationally known education expert of the time, visited the Schurz home. She was so impressed with Agathe's achievements she spread the concept of kindergarten nationwide.[2]

At this time, U. S. kindergartens were conducted in German. After visiting European kindergartens and training under Froebel's widow Luise, Ms. Peabody opened the first English-language kindergarten in Boston in 1860.

Public Kindergarten

The first public kindergarten opened in 1873 in St. Louis with 20 children. Kindergarten spread quickly. By 1873, 7,800 five-year-olds were in the St. Louis kindergartens alone. The concept was gaining ground so rapidly the National Education Association established the Department of Kindergarten Education in 1884 and recommended kindergartens in all public schools. By the beginning of the twentieth century, kindergartens had become an integral part of the public school system.

California enacted one of its first laws concerning kindergarten in the 1890s. In 1890 the Los Angeles school board sponsored an amendment to the city charter that allowed public funding of kindergartens. That year the school board took over three private kindergartens and established five more.

In response, the state enacted a law allowing four- and five-year-olds attend public kindergartens, where public programs were offered, in 1891. Kindergarten programs were not funded by the state until an amendment to the California Constitution was passed in 1941.

Even with the rapid rise of kindergarten, they were still based on play and were not compulsory. It would be decades before serious academics became the purpose of early education.

Nursery Schools

During this same time nursery schools were getting a start. Like the early kindergartens, these schools were not intended for academics. Instead they were developed to be childcare opportunities for working parents. Nursery schools were the precursor of what we now know as preschool.

Also in the early 1900s, Italian physician Maria Montessori was developing another philosophy of early childhood education. Dr. Montessori didn't advocate formal learning as seen in today's preschool. She believed children could learn from watching adults model and by having adult equipment made child-sized. For two- to three-year-olds, the emphasis is on physical, motor, and social skills—not academics. The Montessori Method has since become one of the most well-known preschool systems with schools around the world utilizing it.

One of the earliest nursery schools began in 1916 in Chicago. Mrs. Frank R. Lillie started this cooperative of four women. These women wanted to volunteer in the war effort. The "school" consisted of one of the women caring for all the children while the other three volunteered at various agencies. This first effort has grown to what is now the University of Chicago Nursery School. This program, although not the co-op it once was, is still part of the University's Laboratory Schools. It maintains that the philosophy play is learning—play to learn, learn to play.[3]

The same year another nursery school started in New York City at the now famous Bank Street School. Lucy Sprague Mitchell, the first dean of women at the University of California at Berkeley, set up the Bureau of Educational Experiments. Ms. Mitchell's intention was to research educational methods for children.[4]

Philosophy Changes

Like many of the educational changes at the time, Ms. Mitchell's basic philosophy was based on John Dewey's ideas. He believed schools were not just a place of learning, but also a vehicle of social change. Dewey said, "I believe that education is the fundamental method of social progress and reform."[5]

Dewey is thought to be the principal writer of the Humanist Manifesto. His idea of social progress and reform was to turn children from the traditions taught by their families to creatures governed by society. Even as Dewey's progressive education ideas proliferated in American education, it was still rare for young children to attend nursery school.

In the 1930s, Roosevelt's Public Works Administration (PWA) opened nursery schools to provide unemployed teachers with jobs. The Lanham

Act of 1942 funded day care centers for working mothers. These nursery schools and centers were conveniently located in public school buildings. This key placement began the perception that preschool and kindergarten were an integral part of a child's education.

Opposition to these programs was considerable. With the prevailing belief that young children belong with their mothers, one reason for the opposition was that the programs sparked visions of children abandoned in orphanages. After World War II these schools and centers were closed.

Head Start

Not until the 1960s, with the advent of Head Start and more women entering the workforce, did sending young children away from home become a trend. With that trend, even families in which mothers were not employed began to think that preschools were desirable, even necessary, for their child's future success.

Head Start began in 1965 as a part of President Lyndon Johnson's war on poverty. The idea behind this program was to provide education, health, and social services to preschool-aged children from low-income families. Johnson, who at one time taught in a Texas one-room schoolhouse, believed education to be the way out of poverty.

The Head Start program was modeled on British infant schools. Robert Owen started British infant schools in 1816 in Scotland. He believed children's character could be molded by adults and should be molded in the way society needed or wanted. Owen's concept was to overcome evil by implanting good in children beginning early in life. Head Start has become the model for all preschools today. Consequently, the British infant school philosophy prevails in all preschools today.

In its first year Head Start was an eight-week summer program, directed entirely by volunteers. It was created for three- and four-year-olds who lived in homes at or below the poverty level. The original design was to teach these children necessary skills needed for elementary schools.

The program expanded to a full-day, full-year program. It's grown from an all-volunteer system to an industry that in fiscal year 2007 employed nearly a quarter million in over 18,000 centers around the nation. Funding for Head Start is federal grants authorized each year by Congress and given to non-profit and for-profit organizations.

Head Start was originally intended for three- and four-year-olds, in 1994 the grants were expanded to include Early Head Start to serve infants from birth to age three. In 2007, 10% of Head Start participants were under the age of three.[6]

Program expansions have brought more professional qualifications to those who work with Head Start. By 2013, half of all Head Start teachers must have a BA and all must have at least an AA. These qualifications have given the false impression that special training is needed to care for and teach preschoolers.

Head Start was the beginning of academic preschools. The programs provided through Head Start, both academic and social, are guided by federally mandated standards. The standards for Head Start have become the de-facto standards for all preschools. As a result, parents have come to believe their preschooler must meet the same standards. And the only place these standards can be met is in a preschool program.

No Child Left Behind

No Child Left Behind (NCLB), passed in 2002, became President George W. Bush's signature education program. Preschool recommendations were added in 2004, continuing the march of academic programs for younger children.

These guidelines define a preschool as "a program of educational services for eligible children below the age at which the LEA (local education agencies) provides elementary education and is focused on raising the academic achievement of children once they reach school age [Section 1115(b)(1)(A)(ii), ESEA]." Officially preschool became an academic program.

Preschool children are defined as "… children from birth to the age that the LEA (local education agencies) provides a free public elementary education. Section 1115(b)(1)(A)(ii), ESEA]." Now, a child is considered a preschooler at birth needing a formal academic program to be ready to learn at the age of five.

Being ready-to-learn has come to mean five-year-olds will enter kindergarten with skills that were once taught in first grade. As more pressure is put on schools to increase academics at younger ages, more pressure is put on parents who think they are failing their children without early formal schooling. The NCLB preschool recommendations set the stage for the 2006 Universal Preschool (UP) initiative in California. This is when parents of preschoolers were really put on the spot.

Universal Preschool

The Campaign for UP promised such things as children who go to preschool won't commit crimes and will help save Social Security. Parents were led to believe they would fail their children and contribute to the downfall of society if preschool-aged children weren't enrolled in a formal preschool.

Even parents who had been homeschooling for a number of years began to wonder if all the slogans and studies were correct. So-called authorities, such as First 5, claim "children who attend a quality preschool do better in elementary school"[7] or that preschool increases a child's later success at getting a job. Parents doubt their ability to provide the same quality.

They began looking for preschool curriculum. Some parents have even sent their little ones to a formal preschool program before starting to homeschool kindergarten.

The Universal Preschool movement has spawned the government programs Early Head Start and Zero to Three to begin "teaching" children from birth.

9

Although not as prevalent, parents are now beginning to believe they must begin formal academics before their child is even potty-trained. An entire commercial industry has started to grow up around this idea.

Guidelines for and public information about preschool and early childhood education give lip service to parent involvement. Many recommend that parents be "taught" to help their own little ones. California's First 5 website has a parents' section, which claims to have "what you [the parent] need to know about my health, education, and the services and support you need to raise a happy and healthy me."[8]

When the message is parents aren't capable of raising and teaching the child God gave them, is it any wonder parents have lost confidence in their own ability?

REFERENCES

1. the encyclopedia of informal education, "Frederick Froebel and informal education," http://www.infed.org/thinkers/et-froeb.htm.
2. Wikipedia, "Margarethe Schurz," http://en.wikipedia.org/wiki/Margarethe_Schurz.
3. University of Chicago Laboratory School, "History of the Nursery School," http://www.ucls.uchicago.edu/about-ucls/history/historical-notes/history-of-the-nursery-school/index.aspx.
4. Bank Street School, "Bank Street School of Education: About the School: History," http://www.bankstreet.edu/discover-bankstreet/history.html.
5. Dewey, John, "My Pedagogic Creed," School Journal 54 (January 1897), 77-80, http://dewey.pragmatism.org/creed.htm.
6. The Early Head Start National Resource Center, "What is Early Head Start?" http://www.ehsnrc.org/AboutUs/ehs.htm.
7. First 5 California, "Power of Preschool," California Children & Families Commission, http://www.ccfc.ca.gov/Help/preschool.asp.
8. First 5 Parent Site, California Children & Families Commission, http://www.ccfc.ca.gov/parents/1.

2

The Real Numbers

"Preschool helps children learn to read by third grade."

"Children who attend preschool are more likely to go to college."

"Children who attend preschool are more successful as adults."

With headlines like these, is it any wonder the public in general and parents in particular are convinced young children need some type of formal instruction during the first five years? It is also easy to think the studies and reports quoted are conclusive because opposing reports receive little publicity.

Questionable Claims

These questionable claims were blasted at parents in 2006 when the Preschool For All initiative was on the California ballot. Voters saw through the hyperbole and struck down the attempt at universal preschool.

The headlines, though, struck fear in the hearts and minds of many good parents. Fear they would ruin their children's lives if some type of preschool program wasn't provided, whether at a center or in the home.

Most of the claims made by the Preschool for All (universal preschool) supporters are based on two Rand Corporation reports. The supporters of the Preschool for All initiative commissioned the reports. But, even those reports showed fallacies to the boldly stated claims.

The Rand reports were not based on original research. Instead, they were compiled from the Chicago Child/Parent Program (CPC), a longitudinal study of 1550 children: 1,000 who attended the program and 550 who did not. Rand extrapolated the statistics from the CPC research to children in the state of California. Several problems crop up.

The CPC is not a preschool as we commonly think of preschool. It is a parent and child program. In addition to the child centers, CPC has parent classes, assists parents in finishing their high school diplomas, and conducts in-home visits. Also, parents take part in the preschool center with their children and go on field trips. CPC is more of an outreach program than standard preschool.

CPC is specific to disadvantaged children. Although Rand tries to extend the information to middle class and wealthy children, by their own admission there is little information to make those conclusions.

"On the surface the Rand study looks like a credible, thoroughly research document," said Chris Cardiff, who teaches economics at San Jose State University and is co-author of the analysis of Rand's universal preschool study. "But upon review we found the Rand study fails to pass even the basic benchmarks of what can be considered a reasonable economic analysis."[1]

Broad Generalizations - Narrow Fields

Another problem with many of the studies done on preschool education is the broad generalizations made from a narrow field. Most research is based on Head Start, a program specifically targeting "disadvantaged" or "at risk" children. Dr. David Elkind of Tufts University and Edward F. Zigler of Yale University calls these "inappropriate generalizations" of excellent programs, which are aimed at economically disadvantaged children. These generalizations may not apply to all children. Little evidence is available that shows young children from middle- and high-income homes have the same or any additional advantages.[2]

Since Head Start has become the gold standard for early childhood education, it has been used as "proof" that all young children need some type of formal program. Here again, the reports don't bear out this "fact."

The U.S. General Accounting Office (GAO) has concluded in a number of reports to Congress that Head Start does not produce any long-term advantages for children in the program. All you have to do is read the titles of these reports to get an idea of what is the reality of Head Start. Here are just a few of the reports:

HEAD START: Research Provides Little Information on Impact of Program (April 1997)
Although an extensive body of literature exists on Head Start, only a small part of this

literature is program impact research. This body of research is inadequate for use in drawing conclusions about the impact of the national program in any area in which Head Start provides services such as school readiness or health-related services.

HEAD START: Research Insufficient to Assess Program Impact (March 1998)

In summary, the Head Start program has provided comprehensive services to millions of low-income children and their families—services that in the program's early years participants probably would not have otherwise received. Little is known, however, about whether the program has achieved its goals. Although an extensive body of literature exists on Head Start, only a small part of that involves program impact research. Because of these research studies' individual and collective limitations, this body of research is insufficient for use in drawing conclusions about the impact of the national program.

TITLE I PRESCHOOL EDUCATION: More Children Served, but Gauging Effect on School Readiness Difficult (September 2000)

Currently, <the Department of> Education lacks the information to measure Title I's effect on children's school readiness, . . . Title I funds represent a significant and growing federal investment in preschool education, but its effect on children's school readiness is not known. Given previous difficulties in evaluating the effect of title I funding on older children, questions remain about whether title I's effect on school readiness can be isolated.

With so little known about the impact of Head Start and other early education programs, it is easy to conclude that maybe the statements made about the need for formal, out-of-home programs for children based on Head Start are exaggerated.

Economic Benefits?

The oft-quoted Rand study looks almost exclusively at economic benefits. These claims of "benefits" permeate the thinking of other areas of our society. For example, a 2005 Zogby poll shows that a clear majority of businesses favor publicly supported pre-kindergarten.

However, another conclusion of this poll says, "Business leaders **clearly tie their support to studies** that showed significant economic advantages to providing pre-school to all children. More than four in five say they are more likely to support universal pre-school **because of studies** that showed disadvantaged children provided with pre-K educations *earned higher incomes . . .*" (emphasis added).[3]

Other Research

There is more to the story than these government studies and reports. Extensive research has been conducted with results that are contrary to the widely reported information. Durham University's (England) Curriculum, Evaluation and Management Centre (CEM) conducted one such study.

The CEM study looked at 35,000 children over six years. The results were disappointing to the proponents of early childhood education. In spite of the money spent on and changes made in programs for young children, "children's development and skills at the start of school are no different now than they were before the introduction of the early childhood curriculum."[4]

Various studies have concluded that although children who have been in academic settings for preschool, often called pre-kindergarten, start kindergarten with an academic advantage, the advantage is gone as early as mid-first grade. The cost of this short-lived academic advantage is increased discipline and behavior problems, the least reported outcome of early formal pre-kindergarten programs

Experts agree that children learn aggressive behavior or control of aggressive behavior during the first five years. As young as 18 months, a child can begin to imitate destructive actions. [5] Although cognitive gains may be seen with higher reading and math scores, the cost is a negative impact on social behavior. These negative behaviors were greater when children entered a care center at a younger age.[6]

Brain Science

Brain science is also invoked as a reason for earlier and earlier formal education programs. It is this "science" that has led to the development of such in-home programs as Little Einstein. The advancements in neurobiology do provide a wealth of information about how and when the brain learns. The very young brain, birth to five years, develops rapidly, more rapidly than at any other time in life. This information has led to the mistaken belief that programs need to be in place to capture this rapid learning phase. The programs to capture this development phase have focused on reading and writing at the expense of social play and child-directed exploration.

Jennifer Matthews looked at various research reports and compiled the conclusions of these reports in her paper "Early Brain Development Research: Implications on Early Childhood Education." She found little support for early group or classroom experiences to nurture the rapid development of a young child's brain. In fact, some of the conclusions drawn are quite the opposite.

Ms. Matthews found research indicates that

- Secure attachments and relationships are more important than curriculum
- An environment of learning is more important than curriculum
- Infants and young children are active and self-motivated learners
- Although the brain develops and grows rapidly during the first five years of life, it is never too late for a child to learn

- Each child is unique and learns differently.
- Brain studies should not be used to promote or market "smarter baby"materials.[7]

In his book *The Myth of the First Three Years,* John T. Bruer discusses the use of brain science to set early childhood policy and says, "... it seemed as if there was, in fact, no new brain science involved in the policy and media discussions of child development. What seemed to be happening was that selected pieces of rather old brain science were being used, and often misinterpreted, to support preexisting views about child development and early childhood policy."[8]

Something is Missing

In all the studies done on young children, there is one key element missing: families. Certain assumptions are made about children in the preschool age group. One is that no parent or other family is available to care for the children in a home environment. Again, economics is the basis for the rational. The reasoning is families "need" two incomes, therefore all families have two working parents, and therefore all children are placed in a center for care.

Supporters of universal preschool base this argument on statements like this one from Vermont state legislator Bill Suchmann: "Many children do not have parents available at home or even capable of appropriate intellectual stimulation."[9] Mr. Suchmann is quoted often, with no factual foundation for his statement. No study can be found that looks at children who remain home with a parent or are in the care of another family member.

Social Experiment

Dr. Molly H. Minkkinen of the University of Minnesota, Duluth, wrote in the *Journal of College Teaching and Learning*, "Today children in the United States are living a social experiment with unknown consequences." She also stated, "A large number of today's children spend their days with people who do not love them unconditionally, people who come and go from their lives at a time when their brains are organizing attachment patterns."

But Dr. Minkkinen sadly concludes that child care for young children needs to be improved rather than children spending more time with loving family members.[10]

The high profile reporting of a few questionable statements from research have parents of young children thinking that they are failing their child. The leap is to put young children in preschool programs, even if the intention is to homeschool later. Few parents want to think that they are hindering their child's chances for success as an adult.

References

1. "Professors Find Preschool Benefits Grossly Exaggerated," May 20, 2006, Reason Foundation, http://www.reason.org/news/show/126869.html.
2. Elkind, David, *Miseducation: Preschoolers at Risk* (1987; New York: Knopf, 1997), 69, and Edward F. Zigler, "Formal Schooling for Four-Year-Olds?", 28.
3. Peck, Christian W., "American Business Leaders' Views On Publicly-funded Pre-kindergarten and the Advantages to the Economy," Zogby International, December 2005, 3.
4. Weston, John-Henry, "Massive Study Finds Pre-School and Early Child Education Initiatives Show No Benefit," August 2007, accessed April 8, 2010, http://www.lifesitenews.com/ldn/2007/aug/0708 31.htm#5.
5. Keenan, Kate, "The development and socialization of aggression during the first five years of life," Encyclopedia on Early Childhood Development, http://www.child-encyclopedia.com/en-ca/child-aggression/according-to-experts/keenan.html.
6. Tremblay, Richard E., "Development of physical aggression from early childhood to adulthood," Encyclopedia on Early Childhood Development, http://www.child-encyclopedia.com/en-ca/child-aggression/according-to-experts/tremblay.html.
7. Matthews, Jennifer (June 23, 2005), *Early Brain Development Research: Implications for Early Childhood Education*, 6.
8. Bruer, John T, *The Myth of the First Three Years: A New Understanding of Early Brain*

Development and Lifelong Learning, 1999 The Freepress, 3.

9. Suchmann, Bill, "Not Mandatory," Letter to the editor, Burlington Free Press, March 8, 1998.
10. Minkkinen, Molly H., Marchel, Mary Ann and Riordan, Kim (2006), Kindergarten Readiness: The Changing Focus of Childhood, University of Minnesota Duluth, http://www.d.umn.edu/~mminkkin (accessed May 13, 2009, site now discontinued).

3

What Experts Say

"I'm not going back," my eight-year-old son announced when we got in the car after church. When I questioned him about his determination, I learned that his Sunday School teacher required him to read aloud. My eight-year-old didn't read well. He was embarrassed and I was sympathetic to his cause.

If this scene were playing out in many homes now, the parents would panic. The Sunday School teacher might even confront the boy's parents about his lack of education. In extreme cases the child welfare department might be contacted about educational neglect.

While my son didn't read on an arbitrary reading level, he was learning. He hadn't reached a level of maturity that he needed to master the complex skill of reading. His maturity level came at about the age of twelve.

Popular opinion has become that a child who isn't reading by the age of eight has either been failed or has a learning disability. To avoid both of these "problems" parents are being encouraged by researchers and politicians to begin education earlier and earlier.

Too Early

Dr. Raymond Moore and his wife Dorothy, often considered one of the pioneers of the modern homeschool movement, became concerned about this trend in the 1960s. They began to conduct research and look at the research of others to find evidence that early school entrance lived up to the claims of early academic achievement. The Moores found that research didn't match the claims.

After the initial research, the Moores and others, through the Hewitt Research Foundation, started to look at what was the best age to start school. The conclusion was that children are better off waiting until the eight to ten before beginning formal academics.[1]

Young Children and Learning

Before becoming concerned about whether you are failing your preschooler academically, let's look at what experts say about young children and learning.

David Elkind, Ph. D, Professor Emeritus of Child Development at Tufts University has written extensively on pushing children to grow up too soon. His peers considered his book, *The Hurried Child*, pop-psychology when it was written in 1981. Dr. Elkind recently wrote about academics over character on his blog, *Digital Children*. He says, "An emphasis upon intellectual achievement and academic success without an equal emphasis on virtue is one-sided and can work against the common good."[2]

Infant and Childhood Development

There is more to infant and early childhood development than just learning to read and cipher.

Children don't learn virtue from sitting at a table drawing letters or counting blocks.

The earliest nursery schools, which produced well-rounded students, were based on play or learning through play. It appears impossible to find a preschool textbook before the 1960s, or even a teacher's guide for preschools that is based on formal academic work. For that matter, pre-1960 preschools had little or no academics. It was a time of play and social interaction. Often these preschools were parent-directed without a "teacher."

Study after study shows that young children learn through interaction with parents (or other caregivers) and play. The studies that have garnered the popular slogans say little about academic growth and nothing about character development.

The National Institute of Child Health and Development, a part of the National Institute for Health, has done studies on the effects of child care on development over the course of more than twenty years. One of the more recent studies makes the following statement:

> Even though child care quality was associated with cognitive and language development, the link was not a strong one. Family and parent features were more important predictors of this development than child care quality.[3]

The findings seem to be clear that family and parent influence is more important than outside influence. If that's the case, why pressure to send children away from home during these formative years?

Socialization?

What about socialization? This question comes up even with preschoolers. Don't children need to be with people other than one or two parents, especially other children the same age, to learn to share, talk, and perform other social activities?

Dr. Moore and his research associates looked at this concern as well. They found that children who spend less time with their parents, and more time with peers, are peer-dependent. This trend has moved down to the preschool ages. Moore's research confirms what many parents truly believe, that children are not best socialized by other children, but rather by the warm, loving adults in their lives.[4]

The National Scientific Council on the Developing Child looks at the science of early childhood relationships. Some of the conclusions are that there is no scientific basis for the belief that multiple adult relationships provides valuable learning experiences. In fact, there are indications that "attaching" and "detaching," along with prolonged separation from familiar caregivers is emotionally distressing and leads to enduring problems.[5]

One argument here is that as long as the young child is with the same daily caregiver, there will be no problem. However does any parent want their young child bonded to another adult in this way?

The same study also says

Children who have healthy relationships with their mothers are more likely to develop insights into other people's feelings, needs, and thoughts, which form a foundation for cooperative interactions with others and an emerging conscience.
When considered within the context of a child's environment of relationships, the concept of school readiness is not exclusively a matter of fostering literacy and number skills but must also include the capacity to form and sustain positive relationships with teachers, children, and other adults, and develop the social and emotional skills for cooperating with others.[6]

This study looked at what relationships do to the growth of the brain. Secure emotional relationships contribute to the healthy development of the brain. Rather than looking at the academics of preschool years, we should be looking at relationships as the key to later academic development. A child who can read, write, and cipher at five, but can't share or speak kindly is going to have problems later on. Now, *there's* scientific evidence.

Need to Be Secure

Dr. Susan B. Campbell in *Advances in Clinical Child Psychology*[7] discusses the need infants and toddlers have for stable and protective relationships with parents. Infants have a need to be secure. When this relationship is fragmented, either through poor parenting skills or multiple caregivers, the result is a child who has missed important attachments and security. This may manifest later in behavior problems; behavior problems that may last a lifetime.

William C. Crain says in the Introduction of his book *Reclaiming Childhood*, "We are so preoccupied with their future that we cannot see or value them for who they are, children" and "All of this adult anxiety about children's future is affecting children's emotional well-being."[8]

The Gesell Institute for Human Development has been looking at childhood development since its inception in 1911 by Dr. Arnold Gesell. Dr. Gesell, working at Yale University, observed developmental stages of children. His stages have been the foundational in child rearing and education.

The Gesell stages are not rigid. All children are unique and develop at their own pace, with ups and downs within each stage. The stages may develop within certain age ranges; they are a natural process, which is different for each child. It is the rare parent who will say, "You are eighteen months old, now walk." It is not unusual, however, in our society to conclude that upon turning five, a child can begin the process of academic learning. And that age is getting lower.

The Institute tells parents that they can provide experiences that help a child develop within each stage, but the rate of growth cannot be speeded up. Parents, or teachers, should not try to push development more quickly – no matter the child's age.

The Institute gives the same warning to preschools.[9]

Trust Yourself

Although preschools may prepare children for the function of school – sitting quietly, following directions, doing worksheets – the experience doesn't necessarily speed learning development.

In a Fall 2009 article, "The Goldilocks Dilemma: What is the 'right time' to start kindergarten?" authors Marcy Guddemmi and Crista Marchesseault lament that legislation, such as No Child Left Behind, has forced more focus on academics with greater accountability and testing, even in early grades. This focus diverts attention away from the appropriate development of children.[10]

Dr. Benjamin Spock, whose book *Baby and Child Care* became the parenting bible of the 1950s and 1960s, often told mothers to "Trust yourself, you know more than you think you do." In other words, it's not what he or other experts say is best for children, it's what you know is best for your child.

I trusted my instinct with my son when he was learning to read, and that instinct proved correct. He learned to read on his terms and in his way without an early childhood education experience.

References

1. Moore Homeschooling, "The Moore Formula," http://www.moorefoundation.com/article.php?id=5.
2. Elkind, David, "Ruminations on the IQ and Virtue," Psychology Today, http://blogs.psychologytoday.com/blog/digital-children/200805/ruminations-the-iq-and-virtue.
3. Eunice Kennedy Shriver National Institute of Child Health and Human Development, NIH, DHHS. (2006). "The NICHD Study of Early Child Care and Youth Development (SECCYD): Findings for Children up to Age 4 1/2 Years (05-4318)," Washington, DC: U.S. Government Printing Office.
4. Moore Homeschooling, "Synopsis," http://www.moorefoundation.com/article.php?id=50
5. National Scientific Council on the Developing Child, "Young Children Develop in an Environment of Relationships," Center on the Developing Child at Harvard University, 2004.
6. Ibid.
7. Campbell, Susan B., "Behavior Problems in Preschool Children: Development and Family Issues," *Advances in Clinical Child Psychology, Vol. 19*, edited by Thomas H. Ollendick, Ronald J. Prinz, Plenum Press, 1977.
8. Crain, William C., *Reclaiming Childhood, Letting Children Be Children in Our Achievement-Oriented Society*, Henry Holt & Co., 2003, 6.
9. Gesell Institute, "Questions Parents Ask," http://www.gesellinstitute.org/parentquestions.html.

10. Guddemmi, Marcy and Marchesseault, Crista, "The Goldilocks Dilemma: What is the 'right time' to start kindergarten?'" Seen Magazine, Fall 2009.

4

Politics of Preschool

Preschool has another history—a political history—a history that can be traced to the late 1800s. As the political movement has progressed, the purported reasons have changed, the names of programs have changed, but an underlying purpose hasn't. The intent is to remove children from their homes at a younger age, to allow the village to raise the children.

The politics of early childhood education go beyond party lines and liberal/conservative issues. Fundamentally it is what type of society do we want in the United States, independence or nanny-state?

Proponents of pre-kindergarten programs, especially government-funded programs, believe that it is society's responsibility to ensure that children grow up to be good citizens. This idea fosters the argument of government's compelling interest in the upbringing and education of young children.

Opponents of such programs believe families are the best place for children, especially young children, to grow and learn social mores. Yes, they say there's a compelling interest for society that children grow up to be responsible citizens. But, they differ from proponents in who can best provide the upbringing.

Liberal vs. Conservative

For the most part, proponents are seen as liberal and opponents as conservative. An analysis of political effects on preschool done by Andrew Karch at the University of Texas, Austin described states that have highly funded and a high percent of enrollment as those with Democrat or liberal-controlled state houses and governors.[1]

But, the conservative/liberal divide isn't always as clear as Mr. Karch indicates. Conservative presidents, George H.W. Bush and George W. Bush, both had preschool/day care initiatives. These initiatives were in the form of child care and Development Block Grant ($1.4 billion annually) in 1990 for the first President Bush, and George W. integrated preschool programs into the No Child Left Behind Act.

Early Beginnings

Some of the first recorded movements for early childhood education in the 1870s were social causes to help the "poor and wretched" children of San Francisco. Socially prominent citizens financed charity kindergartens as an alternative to growing up on the streets, a worthy cause in any decade.

As early as the 1930s, attempts were made to nationalize kindergarten with the federal government providing funds, while leaving the control to states and local governments.[2] The Roosevelt administration set up emergency nursery schools for needy children. When the idea developed in the Federal Emergency

Relief Agency it was primarily to provide jobs. Lois Meek Stolz, director of Institute for Child Development at Teacher's College, reportedly said, "Who could you employ? Nutritionists, maintenance workers, all kinds of people besides teachers!"[3]

The National Association for Nursery Education (NANE) hoped that emergency nursery schools would become part of the public schools, where many of the programs were located. In 1947 federal funding of kindergarten was defeated for the last time because legislators believed that not only should education, including kindergarten, be left under the jurisdiction of states and local districts but also there was no longer a need since the war was over and mothers were no longer needed in the workforce.[4]

As noted in chapter one, government-funded child care programs were used in the 1940s to allow mothers to work in war effort jobs and provide employment for teachers. These programs were also abandoned quickly after World War II when mothers returned home to raise children.

Resurgence

The decades of 1960s and 1970s saw another resurgence of women in the workforce. This growth was spurred in part by baby-boom children now entering school and eventually by the feminist movement. The perceived need now became child care for the children the millions of working moms.

It was at this time political parties learned that campaigns that put the interest of the children at the forefront were winners. After all, parents want the best for their children, even when proposed programs go against the natural tendency to nurture your own child.

Head Start had already been firmly implanted as an early childhood education program. But it didn't meet the need of middle class working women and was already showing dismal academic results. Walter Mondale (D-MI) led a group of liberal Democrats to expand early childhood programs beyond child care for low-income families. He pushed the Child Development Act through Congress in 1971.

This act would have required government-funded programs to enroll any child regardless of family income or child care need. In Senator Mondale's words, the act provided "a full range of quality health, education, nutrition and social services" for the young.[5] The Child Development Act would have pushed government involvement in the lives of young children far beyond the interest of child care for poor working mothers.

Although the stated reasons were to provide child care for single mothers currently receiving welfare, the act was named to in such a way as to encourage all parents to enroll their children. President Richard Nixon vetoed the bill because it "would commit the vast moral authority of the national Government to the side of communal approaches to child rearing over against the family-centered approach." [6]

Accepting Out-of-Home Care

Even into the 1990s, the American public wasn't prepared to accept that out-of-home child care was good for young children. However studies done in 1999 and 2000 found that people fully accepted the idea of academic achievement for young children as a good reason to send children away from home. Using this information, universal preschool advocates changed the campaign from child care to education, and nursery schools or preschools became more acceptable.[7] The changing of terms has blurred the lines of the arguments. Since academic preschools are now often used as full-day child care, the two have merged in political agendas. The two terms, preschool and child care, are now used interchangeably in the argument.

In general, as you have seen in previous chapters, the arguments in favor of universal preschool have little to do with raising children to become responsible citizens. The studies and publicity have focused on economics. Little information has been disseminated about the studies and anecdotal information that shows early childhood education interferes with the social growth of the child.

Politics of Economics

By focusing research on economic value of pre-K and full-day kindergarten, proponents have been able to convince businesses to support the movement. The National Education Association (NEA) reports and other studies brag about the number of businesses that support pre-K investments (note the word usage: investment vs. spending). Even the Federal Reserve Bank has weighed in.

In the March 2003 of *fedgazzette* from the Federal Reserve Bank of Minnesota, Rob Grunewald, Regional Economic Analyst and Arthur J. Rolnic, Senior Vice President and Director of Research wrote

> A well-managed and well-funded early childhood development program, or ECDP, provides such support. Current ECDPs include home visits as well as center-based programs to supplement and enhance the ability of parents to provide a solid foundation for their children. Some have been initiated on a large scale, such as federally funded Head Start, while other small-scale model programs have been implemented locally, sometimes with relatively high levels of funding per participant.
>
> The question we address is whether the current funding of ECDPs is high enough. We make the case that it is not, and that the benefits achieved from ECDPs far exceed their costs. Indeed, we find that the return to ECDPs far exceeds the return on most projects that are currently funded as economic development.[8]

A 2005 Zogby poll conducted for the Committee for Economic Development showed that four out of five American business leaders agreed that investments in effective preschool programs for children are important for the long-term success of the U.S. economy and that access to quality preschool programs has positive implications for the nation's future workforce. Some 83 percent favor publicly funded pre-kindergarten at the parents' option.[9]

Quality Child Care

A political buzzword in the argument for institutionalizing younger children has become quality—quality child care, quality preschool, quality education. The definition of "quality" reveals the political agenda is something less than the good of the children.

Preschool California lists the following as some of the "hallmarks of high-quality preschool program:"

Teachers
Early childhood education teachers and assistant teachers:
• are expert, *well-trained and have received specialized training* in early childhood education; (emphasis added)

Families
• Family members are engaged in the program through conferences with teachers, opportunities to *assist in the classroom and other activities.* (emphasis added)
• Family members are offered information about nutrition, parenting and social services, when needed.

Comprehensive Care
Programs provide vision, hearing and general-health screenings to identify children's

special needs early and provide appropriate supports and referrals.

    • Children are offered breakfast and/or lunch.[10]

According to Preschool California, the number one indicator of quality is well-trained (read credentialed) teachers. Families are relegated to a secondary position, then only as assistants. They go on to say a quality program provides health care and meals, something that used to be exclusive to the family.

Who supports this "quality"? The National Education Association and California Teachers Association (CTA). Both of which will gain members with the increased requirements of government-funded programs.

Certified Teachers

In the early 20th century, the National Kindergarten Association pushed for credentialed teachers in nursery schools and kindergartens. The federal kindergarten bill in the 1930s included a provision for the kindergartens and nursery schools to be conducted by graduates of courses for teachers at accredited institutions. This bill was ultimately defeated.

The National Education Association has long advocated for publicly funded full-day kindergarten, along with pre-K for all three and four-year-olds. One of their recommendations states, "Public schools should be the primary provider of pre-kindergarten programs, and additional funding must be allocated to finance them in the same manner as K-12 schools."[11]

NEA policy brief "Early Childhood Education and School Readiness" (2008)[12] states,

> NEA urges states to make high-quality early childhood education programs a priority and consider them an integral part of the education continuum. States should encourage and support the efforts of public schools in their efforts to provide early childhood programs.

The same policy brief further extrapolates that credentialed and higher paid teachers make for a better pre-K experience.

Teachers, support professionals, and administrators working at the prekindergarten level should be considered qualified if they hold the license or certification that the state requires for their employment. These educators also should have access to high-quality, continuous, professional development that's required to gain and improve knowledge and skills and that is provided at school district expense.

Better Experience?

What is a better pre-K experience? One example often cited is Oklahoma, which not only has a state-funded universal preschool program, but also requires the teachers have an early childhood certificate. The proof of effectiveness? Seventy percent of Oklahoma's four-year-olds are enrolled in the state-funded system.[13]

While Oklahoma may be recognized as one of the most successful in the nation because of the high percentage of four-year-olds enrolled, the actual educational benefits leave doubt about the real success. According to Alex Cameron in "Oklahoma Gets An 'A' In Early Childhood Education, But An 'F' When It Counts" the supposed benefits in reading and math aren't sustainable.

The most recent National Assessment of Education Progress (NAEP) fourth grade reading and math scores show that the scores of Oklahoma fourth graders, relative to the national average, have declined over the roughly ten-year period since the state became the leader in early childhood education.[14]

The NEA even provides an advocacy guide for full-day kindergarten, which includes policy recommendations and model legislation. The result has been a campaign that has caused parents to question their own natural instincts.

And Today

Today, with the economic crisis, the call has been to help parents look for work or continue in two jobs by providing quality child care. Since businesses have long supported government-funded preschools to have a ready workforce, support for government-funded child care is not a hard leap.[15]

During the Universal Preschool campaign in California, private day care and preschool programs fought against the proposal, expecting that they would lose children due to free care elsewhere. But, the current economic situation may bring these coalitions together. More private preschool may now be willing to accept government funds, and regulations, to be able to stay open.

Parents removing their children from preschools because of the high cost have become another argument for government funding. A November 2008 MSNBC article decried the situation with horror stories of children being left alone in cars while parents worked. Some children are left with grandparents, which according to this story isn't considered quality or adequate.[16]

The response to the MSNBC article from parents, however, indicates that many parents are making other adjustments, like staying home when they can.

One mother wrote:

> I quit my job two years ago to stay at home with my 3 children, the reason? I couldn't afford day care. I was making the same amount as the day care expenses were. ... I noticed a huge behavioral improvement in my oldest son, just months after I quit. He had been in day care from the age of 3 and is now 9. My youngest son, who was in day care since age 3 months, also made a huge improvement.[17]

A father, who said he "daddied up" when his business saw a downturn, said

> One decision I made was to shift my schedule and remove my kids from Day Care (sic)

and care for them myself with the help of my wife who teaches school.

It was tough. I was used to someone else (day care) doing the daytime raising of my kids and not used to my schedule as well as my freedom being uninterrupted by a million questions, dirty diapers and in general someone else's dependence on me. ... . I made it not only work but realized what a fool I'd been to ever cry about my responsibilities to my children. ....They are a blessing I would never have realized had I just got another part-time job or had Clinton came and bailed me out financially and I was "rewarded" by them getting to stay in day care.[18]

Access for All

The Obama administration and Congress are formulating plans to further "help" parents by federally funding child care (preschool) through grants to states. These grants will have no restrictions on income level, so even those who can afford child care will place their children in free programs.

The argument is to ensure all children have access to preschool. However, 80 percent of the nation's four-year-olds and more than half of three-year-olds already attend a preschool program, a substantial portion of these children are in private preschools rather than government-funded programs.

Head Start already provides free services to low-income families. Furthermore, only 16 percent of mothers with young children prefer to work full time, a figure which dropped by half in the ten years from 1997 to 2007.

In the 2009-2010 legislative session, a number of bills, including the cutely named Providing Resources for Kids Early Act (Pre-K Act), were introduced in spite of the information that shows it is unnecessary. Five billion dollars was included in the American Recovery and Reinvestment Act (the stimulus bill) for early childhood education and care.

Where is all of this leading? First, as taxes go up more parents will feel pressure to have both parents work. Thus more young children will need child care. Second, as this created need grows, children will be required to enroll in preschool or pre-kindergarten programs, essentially removing child-rearing rights from parents.

REFERENCES

1. Karch, Andrew, "Divergent Paths: Teacher Qualification Requirements and Classroom Regulations in State Prekindergarten Programs," Paper presented at the 2008 Annual Meeting of the Midwest Political Science Association, Chicago, Il.
2. Devita, Carol J.and Mosher-Williams, eds. *Who Speaks for America's Children? The Role of Child Advocates in Public Policy*, Urban Institute Press, 2001, 173.
3. Beatty, Barbara, *Preschool Education in America: The Culture of the Young Child from the Colonial Era to Present,* 1995 Yale University Press, 177.
4. Ibid.
5. "The Nation: Child Care Veto," Time Magazine, Dec. 20, 1971, http://www.time.com/time/magazine/article/0,91 71,878957,00.html#ixzz0chSAq7l7.
6. Ibid.
7. Devita and Mosher-Williams, *Who Speaks for Children*, 180.
8. Gundewald, Ron and Rolnick, Arthur J., "Early Childhood Development: Economic Development with a High Public Return," f*edgazette*, March 2003
9. Peck, Christian W. "American Business Leaders' Views On Publicly-funded pre-kindergarten and the Advantages to the Economy," 2005, Zogby International.
10. Preschool California, "What is High-Quality Preschool?" Outreach Packet,

http://www.preschoolcalifornia.org/assets/pc-documents/outreach-packet/7-what-is-high-quality-preschool.pdf.

11. National Education Association, "Early Childhood Education," http://www.nea.org/home/18163.htm.

12. Barnett, W. S., Epstein, D. J., Friedman, A. H., Sansanelli, R. A., & Hustedt, J. T. (2009). *The state of preschool 2009: State preschool yearbook.* The National Institute for Early Education Research, Rutgers Graduate School of Education. Retrieved from http://nieer.org/yearbook2009.

13. Cameron, Alex, "Oklahoma Gets An 'A' In Early Childhood Education, But An 'F' When It Counts," News on 6, http://www.newson6.com/Global/story.asp?S=135 33552.

14. National Education Association, *Early Childhood Education and School Readiness*, policy brief, 2008.

15. National Education Association, *NEA on Pre-Kindergarten and Kindergarten*, 2004.

16. Associated Press, "Cash-strapped parents pull kids from day care," Personal Finance, MSNC, 2008, http://www.msnbc.msn.com/id/27597240/?GT1= 43001.

17. Newsvine, "Cash-strapped parents pull kids from day care," comments, 2008, http://kibbitzer.newsvine.com/_news/2008/11/09 /2091747-cash-strapped-parents-pull-kids-from-day-care#comments.

18. Ibid.

5

Lessons from the Bible

What does the Bible say about early childhood education? Not much. As in many areas of our lives, God has not given specific instructions, but He has given us some examples.

When God said to train up a child, do you think He meant academic training? Social training? Or spiritual training?

Early childhood education as we know it today was unheard of even fifty years ago, and certainly not in the time and culture of the Bible. Though we live in a different time and culture, we still need to consider what some parents in the Bible did and how they trained their young children in godly living.

God's Provision

In the few instances of a child being removed from the family of birth, God made provision for the young child to be with his mother until weaning. Tradition puts the age of weaning at somewhere between three and five years old. It was often during this time that these children learned of their parents' faith and God. Moses and Samuel are the two primary examples that show us the importance of the early years for young children.

You may remember Moses' story. At the time of his birth in Egypt, the pharaoh had given orders that newborn male babies were to be killed. Moses was saved from this edict when his mother placed him in a wicker basket, which was set afloat among the reeds along the river edge. Here the pharaoh's daughter found young Moses and adopted him. Through God's providence, Moses was returned to his birth family until he was weaned, then taken to live and grow up in pharaoh's palace (Exodus 2:1-8).

Jocheved knew she only had a short time to instill in her son faith in God. I can imagine that she used every moment to tell Moses about his ancestral roots, the promise God made to Abraham's many descendants and miraculously delivering on that promise, and the power of God. Jocheved used the time, a mere three years, to train him to serve God. We, too, have little time with our children. We must take on the same urgency in training our children to love the Lord.

As the grandson of pharaoh, Moses would have had the finest academic education in Egypt. Although he remained under the influence of Egypt for forty years, he never forgot his Hebrew roots. The website Judaism 101 puts it this way, "Yocheved <sic> instilled in Moses a knowledge of his heritage and a love of his people that could not be erased by the 40 years he spent in the antisemitic <sic> court of Pharaoh."[1] It was the learning at his mother's knee that stuck with him.

Moses didn't forget his mother's training–preschool training if you will. We know he went on to be God's chosen leader to free the Hebrews from Egypt.

Later we learn about Samuel. Hannah offered him into the service of God, even before he was born. Hannah was barren. She cried out to God in her grief and promised to give her child to him. God answered her prayer, and Hannah kept her promise. After Samuel was weaned, she took him to the temple and gave him to God for the rest of his life (I Samuel 1-2).

Hannah spent her time with her son during those early years, even forgoing religious pilgrimages. Although his mother taught Samuel until weaning, unlike Moses, the priest Eli raised him in the temple. It turned out that the temple may have been less than ideal for spiritual training. God calls Eli's sons wicked men and wouldn't allow the priesthood to continue in that family. Samuel, on the other hand, grew in stature and in favor with God (I Samuel 2). God chose Samuel, well trained by his mother, to continue the priesthood. Samuel is considered the last judge and first prophet of God.

First Priority

For the Christian parent, raising children who love and serve God should be the first priority. The admonition in Deuteronomy 6:6-8 to impress God's decrees on our children, isn't just for school-aged children—it is for all, including our preschoolers. God explains why we live by and teach our children God's decrees: because they haven't lived long enough to see God's work in action (Deut. 11:2). Therefore, even our youngest children need to see and hear God in us.

Matthew Henry says in his *Concise Commentary on the Bible*, "Little children should be taught to worship God when very young. Their parents should teach them in it, bring them to it, and put them on doing it as well as they can; God will graciously accept them, and will teach them to do better."[2]

The teaching of spiritual truths begins early and expands as our children grow. Samuel spent about ten years under the teaching of Eli, serving in the temple, observing other adults before God spoke to him. Samuel had been prepared from infancy to be sensitive to the voice of God. When God spoke his call for Samuel, Samuel was ready to listen. What started in infancy continued through his childhood and on into adulthood. He was recognized by all of Israel as a prophet of God (I Samuel 3:20).

Paul points out the importance of early spiritual training at home. In the book of 2 Timothy, he tells Timothy that his faith began with the faith of his grandmother and mother (1:5). Later, Paul reminds Timothy that he was taught the Scriptures from *infancy*, which led to his salvation (3:15).

Ready to Learn Jesus

If there's any credence to the idea that the first years of brain growth are the most important for learning, then these early years must be used to teach about God. Again, from Matthew Henry, "As soon as possible every child should be led to the knowledge of the Saviour."[3]

Advocates of early childhood education use mottos such as "Every child should be ready to learn." Although it sounds admirable, aren't all children born ready to learn? As parents we should be concerned more about *what* they are learning, rather than fulfilling a slogan. What is it you want your child to learn and retain throughout life? That's what you should teach during the early years.

Do we become so concerned about the academic and social training of our children that we forget about the spiritual training? When your purpose is to raise your children to become godly adults, academics, though essential, become secondary. The question should not be, is my child ready for school, but rather, is my child ready for heaven?

When we change our thinking from academic preparation to spiritual preparation first, the issues of preschool change drastically. Instead of worrying about whether our preschoolers are "ready to learn," we concern ourselves with whether they know how to speak to God and hear from him.

Does this mean we ignore the academic subjects? No. We know Jesus learned to read Hebrew and debate before the age of twelve (Luke 2: 40-53). He could not have questioned and amazed the priest had he not known the Scriptures. Learning to read, write, and study other academic subjects is important for a Christian to follow God's will. But academic subjects are not the primary principles to teach during the early impressionable years.

My youngest son came to me when he was five years old with his Bible. He read, "In the beginning, God created the heaven and earth." I hadn't spent dedicated time teaching him phonics or reading.

But, by reading God's Word, I did teach him about God and how to hide God's Word in his heart. The actual reading was an outgrowth of his spiritual education. God gave to my son what was needed to hear him.

Each family will have a different experience with its young children. God will train each, through mother and father, in a different way, for a different and unique plan. By choosing spiritual living and lessons as our top priority from infancy on, just as God gave Samuel ears to hear when he called, God will give our sons and daughters ears to hear as well.

REFERENCES

1. Rich,Tracey R. "Judaism 101, Moses, Aaron, and Miriam," http://www.jewfaq.org/moshe.htm.
2. Henry, Matthew, *Concise Commentary on the Bible,* "I Samuel," http://www.biblegateway.com/resources/commentaries/Matthew-Henry/1Sam/Samuel-Hannah-Presents-Lord.
3. Ibid.

6

Let Them Play

For most of us, our first memories begin at about the age of five. Think about your earliest memories. Aren't they happy events, maybe with siblings and parents playing a silly game or camping in the backyard? Now try to recall your first schooling memories. Do you immediately see yourself sitting at a table drawing letters and numbers? Or are the memories of playing, such as a game of tag or on the playground swinging so high your feet touch the sky?

When I think back to my kindergarten experience I think of playing in the little kindergarten playground, sitting on a rug to listen to the teacher read, and at an easel painting. I have to really work hard to remember academic activities. Certainly there must have some because I learned to count and write my name. Or maybe my mother taught me those things, and I don't remember because it was a natural experience.

Why is it that most of us remember fun and games of childhood, rather than the drudgery of workbooks? I think it's because fun sticks with us, not what is boring. In focusing on teaching reading, writing, and arithmetic at younger and younger ages, many have forgotten the importance of play.

Play, Work, Learn

Play is a child's work. Play is a child's way of learning. Far too many parents and educators believe Jean Piaget's theory of play: play is for pleasure and is based on what is previously learned. Piaget didn't think play necessarily teaches anything new. But studies are proving that Piaget was wrong.[1]

The reliance on Piaget's theory of play has been in part responsible for changes in the preschool and kindergarten classrooms. The other part is the push for academic results, even testing, at the end of preschool or pre-kindergarten programs. Play-oriented preschools programs, or programs where the child is allowed to initiate learning experiences through play, are being changed to academic-oriented programs, where learning experiences are initiated by the teacher using a set standard or curriculum. The change is taking place in spite of research that indicates academic preschools do not produce lasting academic results.

Play vs. Academic

Germany began the move from play-oriented kindergartens to academic-oriented kindergartens in the 1970s. During that time a comparison study was done of 100 kindergartens, fifty of which were play-oriented and fifty that were academic-oriented. The children were followed until the fourth grade. The children who began their education in a play-oriented kindergarten not only excelled in academic development, but also in physical, emotional, and social development. The difference was most striking among children from low-income families.

A more recent study (2002) conducted by Rebecca Marcon of the University of North Florida found similar results. Ms. Marcon's studied followed children from three types of preschool environments: academic-oriented, play-oriented (Marcon labels these as child-initiated), and middle-of-road, which uses a combination of both. At the end of the children's fifth year of school, there was no difference in academic performance. But at the end of the sixth year of school, children in the play-oriented earned significantly higher grades. Students in middle-of-the road had no significant differences from those in an academic program.

Ms. Macron's research also indicates that children in the academic-oriented programs lagged behind in social development. She also hints at what every mother of boys knows, young boys learn better in an active, hands-on enviroment.[2]

In Germany the response to such research was to return to play-oriented kindergartens. In her paper "The Vital Role of Play in Early Childhood Education," Joan Almon says ". . . it is alarming that play has lost so much ground in young children's lives during the past thirty years."[3]

Even more interesting is a study done in Michigan which compared at students, ages three to four years old, in two play-oriented programs and one academic-oriented program. I.Q. scores of all three programs rose, nearly thirty points higher than average scores. These students were followed until the age of twenty-three and the social indicators were very telling.

By the age of fifteen, students from the play-oriented schools had half as many delinquencies as those from the academic-oriented program. Further along, at age twenty-three, the play-oriented students had fewer felony arrests and fewer hours in special education for emotional impairment.[4]

Grim Outlook for Play

Since that time things have become grimmer with full-day kindergartens, lower compulsory attendance age, and, at the beginning of 2010, recommended national academic standards put forth by governors and state superintendents of schools. These recommendations were accepted by more states in order to receive more federal education money.

The new standards seem to take the delight out of learning. Here are some examples of kindergarten standards for English language:

- Name the author and illustrator of a text and define the role of each in presenting the ideas or information in a text.
- Compare and contrast the most important points and key details presented in two texts on the same topic.
- Read emergent-reader texts with purpose and understanding.
- Create engaging audio recordings of stories or poems that demonstrate fluid reading at

an understandable pace; add visual displays when appropriate to emphasize or enhance certain facts or details.[5]

There are other standards that deal exclusively with facts and sequences. None about imaginative stories that young children love to create.

Imagination and Pretend

Free and imaginative playtime has educational benefits that are rarely reported. Sara Smilansky, an Israeli psychologist, conducted studies during the 1960s and 70s. She looked at the sociodramatic play of three- to six-year olds in Israel and the United States. Smilansky found that not only did this type of play promote positive social development; it also promoted intellectual development as well.

Smilansky examined children's ability to organize and communicate their thoughts. One particular study, which followed the children through second grade, indicated that this type of play developed thinking skills that are important to later academic work. She concludes,

> For example, problem solving in most school subjects requires a great deal of make-believe: visualizing how the Eskimos live, reading stories, imagining a story and writing it down, solving arithmetic problems and determining what will come next. History, geography, and literature are all make believe. All of are

conceptual constructions never directly experienced by the child.[4]

What about adult involvement in children's playtime? Should it be avoided completely? No. Adults can be involved as much as the children want them to be.

One of my sons was a child who was often thought of as "spaced out." He would enter his world of imagination and tune out all that was going on around him. He rarely invited anyone else, other than those in his imagination, to take part in his play.

His daughter on the other hand likes to invite adults to join her. Not particularly to get on the floor and play with her, but to be available when she wants the involvement. She loves to pretend to host a tea party.

She will spend several minutes making tea and snacks, either in the same room as adults or in her bedroom. After the preparation, she serves adults the product of her work. And she does expect a response. It may be as simple as thank you or a complimentary comment about the quality of the tea and snack. After serving each person she wants to, she'll clean up and return to her solitary play. While she invites us into her pretend world, she doesn't want any of us to take over and direct her pretend.

My son learned to think outside of the physical world during his imagination play. As an adult he can now study a problem, seemingly being in another world, and imagine possible solutions. The development of thinking outside of time and space has served him well. And, in spite of what some people may think, my son is not a loner who had to be taught to relate to other people. I believe he developed social skills while playing in an imaginary world.

My granddaughter also plays in an imaginative world. Hers is a little more concrete in that tea parties, serving other people, and cleaning up are all activities that are done by adults. Through her pretend play she is thinking creatively and learning important life skills.

Free Play

All of these numbers and studies don't mean parents or schools should plan more playtime. Planning playtime, in the minds of many adults, means that the adults need to provide the materials, structure, and rules. What children really need is for parents to provide more playtimes for spontaneous and self-directed play.

All too often we adults have our own idea of what is fun and important for children's playtime. And just as often it is not play at all. As we become obsessed with our young children learning, we tend to turn every activity into a learning activity. Of course it's what we have come to equate learning with specific subjects such as reading or math. We forget that learning goes beyond the three Rs.

I admit to getting on the floor with a child to make the play educational. When a child is learning to stack blocks, does knowing the colors of the blocks make a difference? I now know that sometimes I should have stayed in the background.

My granddaughter and I went to a weekly playgroup when she was three and four years old. Generally, the children played at a variety of activities of their own choosing. Some played in small groups; others played by themselves. While the children played, moms visited on the sidelines.

One particular playgroup day, a mom had an idea for the children to make unique gifts for their fathers. Not a bad idea. However, the children were called from their playing to "have fun" making the gift. My granddaughter came when the children were called. The activity intrigued her enough for her to investigate it. But it was not nearly as appealing as the climbing apparatus. My granddaughter, after spending a few minutes on the craft project, was ready to return to the jungle gym. We packed up the supplies to finish the project at home.

Toys

A room full of toys, even educational toys can be overwhelming to a small child. Very young children will move quickly from one activity to another. Having a limited number of choices may help cut down the flurry of activity, which comes from a toddler trying to experience everything. Three- and four-year-olds may become bewildered by so many choices. How many times have you noticed your child has gotten out dozens of toys, one at a time? The toy will hold attention for a short time, and then your child goes on to the next one. This is toy overload. There are just too many things to choose from.

Children want to have free and imaginative play; that is play in which rules are made up and changed as needed. Play that can be taken up and quit at any time. Following examples set by the adults in their lives, children play at real life. A child learns social skills and mores by playing the adult roles that have been modeled in front of them.

Toys labeled as educational aren't always conducive to the type of play that helps a young child learn and mature. Too many of these toys are narrow in the way they can be used and don't really challenge the imagination. Some parents become anxious when a toy isn't being used as the toy company intended, but rather in a way the child finds intriguing.

Toys that require little or no instruction, such as blocks, cars, or dolls, allow for your child to make up games and role-playing activities. With a pile of blocks, your child can build a tower for a while, then move on to creating an airplane, and maybe have a game of matching letters.

When my granddaughter was three, she was fascinated with stair steps and ladders. She experimented with her Legos® to build steps. For several days we had various forms of steps and ladders around the house. She didn't need instructions; instead she wanted to figure it out on her own.

When playtime is structured or guided, that free flow of pretending is lost. The time to practice what they have watched is gone. Think of it this way: It's time for you to relax and someone tells you, "You must do this to relax, and these are the rules you much follow to relax." How relaxed would you feel?

Thus far we've only looked at indoor play. Outdoor play is just as important, and is being changed or abandoned.

Play Outdoors

The reasons for the decline in outdoor play are numerous, including the limiting of playtime in favor of formal academics. Preschools and kindergartens are shortening recess and playtime to meet academic standards.

Since the mid-1980s some states have prescribed such stringent academic standards on kindergarten programs that play has become a casualty. In the state of Pennsylvania, kindergarten teachers are told how many minutes to spend on each subject. One teacher commented, "I break the law every day and let my children play for fifteen minutes." [6]

There was a time in this country when children went out to the backyard in the morning to play and came in for refreshment or a change of activity. In today's culture, children have little opportunity for this kind of free play. One of the reasons is their time is highly scheduled with lessons, soccer practice, play dates, pencil and paper work, church activities, and so on and on.

Children need free time outside, whether it's in the backyard making roads for toy cars or at the playground playing on swings and slides. Playing outdoors offers more room for imaginative play. Even the confines of a backyard are a large world to a three- or four-year-old.

Playing outside gives children needed exercise for healthy bone and muscle growth. Running, jumping, or bounding a ball contribute to the maturity of a child's perceptual motor abilities, balance, and eye-hand coordination—all firm foundations for later academic work. Playing in the sun offers health benefits, such as vitamin D absorption. Playing in the dirt contributes to a healthy immune system.

The hygiene hypothesis states that lack of exposure to germs and bacteria in early childhood contributes to allergies, asthma, and other autoimmune disorders later in life. First given a scientific background by David P. Strachan in an article in the British Medical Journal in 1989.[7] There is now even a website dedicated to the hypothesis (www.hygienehypothesis.com).

Since that time other scientists have studied the hypothesis, and some have drawn a conclusion that we are now keeping children too clean. Dr. Marc McMorris, M.D., a pediatric allergist at the University of Michigan Health System says common sense is needed in allowing children to play outside, get dirty, and in contact with germs.[8]

Organized Sports

Rather than several children getting together in a backyard to play touch football or other impromptu sports, children are now organized into teams and leagues. Have you ever watched a soccer game with five-years-olds on the field? It's great fun. The little ones are usually running helter-skelter after the ball, few staying in their assigned positions. There also seems to be one or two youngsters who are playing their own game, not even related to soccer. By themselves, they may be running in little circles, digging in the grass, or lying down watching the clouds.

Not so fun is watching the adults at such an event. While some parents are enjoying the randomness and inventiveness of the children on the field, others are in a fury. Running up and down the sidelines, they cajole, holler, and in some sad instances threaten when the rules or strategies aren't being followed. When the game is over, some of the children will throw themselves on the ground crying. Not because they've lost the game, but because they have disappointed an adult.

My children played organized sports, but only as long as it was fun for them. And as a parent I was willing to confront an over-zealous coach. Children can learn about teamwork and following rules playing on an organized sports team. When adults take the game too seriously, the sport is no longer a game for children. I think we've all seen a dejected child leave the field when a coach or parent has expressed disappointment.

Young children in sports leagues can be especially vulnerable to feelings of rejection because they lack the maturity to grasp the technicalities of the rules. Four- and five-years-olds want to please adults, especially parents. Even when nothing is directly said, they know when an adult is disappointed. The game is stripped of fun.

Play, indoors and out, offers many benefits emotionally, mentally, and physically for young children. Play also provides the beginnings of good memories that will last a lifetime. What do you want your child's first memory to be? Sitting at a table trying to craft the letters of a word or romping hilariously with you?

REFERENCES

1. Fox, Jill Englebright, Ph. D., "Back-to-Basics: Play in Early Childhood," Early Childhood News, http://www.earlychildhoodnews.com/earlychildhood/article_view.aspx?ArticleID=240.
2. Marcon, Rebecca, "Moving up the Grades: Relationship between Preschool Model and Later School Success," Early Childhood Research and Practice, Vol. 4. No. 1, http://ecrp.uiuc.edu/v4n1/marcon.html.
3. Almon, Joan, *The Vital Role of Play in Early Childhood Education,* Waldorf Early Childhood Association of North America, 2004, http://www.waldorfearlychildhood.org/article.asp?id=5.
4. Ibid.
5. Common Core Standards Initiative, "English Language Arts Standards & Literacy in History/Social Studies, Science, and Technical Studies," 2010, http://www.corestandards.org/assets/CCSSI_ELA%20Standards.pdf.
6. Almon, *The Vital Role of Play in Early Childhood Education.*
7. Strachen, David, "Hay fever, hygiene, and household size," 1989, *British Medical Journal, 299*, 1259-1260
8. University of Michigan Health System. "The Hygiene Hypothesis: Are Cleanlier Lifestyles Causing More Allergies For Kids?" *ScienceDaily,* 9 September 2007. 17 February 2011 http://www.sciencedaily.com/releases/2007/09/070905174501.htm

7

What Do I Do?

When confronted with the idea of not teaching academics in the formative years you may wonder, "Just what do I do?" Being told to "Do what comes naturally" feels like your concerns are being dismissed. But there is truth in that approach.

As with other areas of early childhood, we parents just seem to know what our children need. We know when an infant's cry is distress, hunger, or just a need to be held close. Why is it we don't trust our instincts when it comes to learning needs?

As discussed in a previous chapter, the most important lessons are spiritual lessons. Teaching our children about God from a very early age is the foundation for our children's entire lives. With that in mind, we can put away any notions that we must have an academic program, preschool at home, to help our children learn.

Discipline

Discipline is an important part of early childhood education and a good place to begin. We are told to discipline our children, one of the few commands that God gives to parents (Prov. 13:14, Prov. 29:15, 17). Discipline goes hand-in-hand with spiritual training. Let's be honest, we have to be self-disciplined to obey God. Our little children learn self-discipline as we teach them right from wrong.

Remember correction is loving, immediate, and consistent. And it is hard work for parents because it's easier to overlook minor offenses, especially when others are looking on. Or a tired mom doesn't want to get up and correct her three-year-old one more time. But it is necessary for adequate learning of self-discipline.

Also remember that discipline doesn't produce perfection. It does, however, produce happy children and parents. Mark Benedict writes, "As parents, we should be satisfied when they habitually show respect, have a sincere regard for spiritual things, and demonstrate genuine trust in Christ by appropriate Christian conduct among their friends and peers." [1]

There is no magic formula or set of prescribed steps to have perfectly obedient children. Each child is different; what works for one will not work for another. My son's first child was a good-natured, compliant baby, and still is as she grows older. He and his wife were ready to experience this same joy with their second baby. Almost from birth, baby number two is the very opposite.

My son called both my husband and me early on seeking advice about what to do with this independent, self-willed little girl. Although he was surprised that what worked for his oldest didn't work with the next child, he knew he needed to begin discipline early for the sake of his daughter's future.

Character Training

Learning about God and learning discipline is the beginning of important character training. Dr.

Martin Luther King said, "Intelligence plus *character* — that is the goal of a true education."

Character does not consist of a single statement or a random act; it is those qualities and dispositions that we practice consistently—both good and bad. It's often said character is who we are when no one is looking.

The Center for Character Development defines character as having six pillars: trustworthiness, responsibility, respect, fairness, caring, and citizenship.[2] Others add such things as faith, honesty, and integrity. How do we help our children learn character and what does it have to do with academic learning?

Character training begins as we teach our children to think of others. This includes knowing that there are limits to our own activities. Each time you teach your child "no," you are teaching self-limits or self-discipline. The person who has self-control does not always think will think of others, an outgrowth of this discipline is learning fairness, caring, and honesty.

I see a natural progression in character development: loving, helping, sharing, and giving. Our children need to learn all these during the preschool years.

Love

Love is first learned from parents and other family members. Love is transmitted more than taught. As we love our children, and they see us love each other, love is learned. Learning to care about others is foundational to the other noble character qualities.

Helping

Helping also begins at home. Once walking is mastered, a child can start helping. Children need to be taught that helping others is not for their own benefit, but because other people benefit from it. The simple act of picking up one toy helps someone else. Most of us are aware that children like to help. When my grandchildren are at our house at mealtime, they are all in the kitchen ready to help. I have tasks for each one that suits individual ages. The four-year-old can place the napkins on the table, while the eight-year-old can carefully pour water into glasses. I often hear, "I like to help."

Our children don't need a specific reward for helping. Then it is a job. The payment for helping is seeing how their actions bring joy to someone else. The act of helping should be a reward of its own.

Sharing

Sharing is an act of kindness. Like loving and helping it's about the other person not self. Children can't be forced to share, but they can be taught how to share.

Young children shouldn't be expected to share naturally. To their young minds, when another child plays with their toy, it can mean that they will no longer have that toy. It may take years to teach sharing, depending on the maturity of the child. It's such a foreign concept; you might as well be speaking in a different language when you tell your child to share their belongings.

For very young children the act of sharing starts with playing side by side. The children may all be playing a different game, but they are playing together. Playing together with similar items (like coloring together) is the next step in sharing. Playing games, working puzzles together, or sharing apple slices, are all beginning efforts of letting someone else use something of theirs.

A child may not completely learn to share until the age of seven or eight. But when taught gradually, according to maturity level, it will become an instinctive tendency.

Giving

Finally, giving. Our family has had the practice of something new in, something old out. The closet isn't stuffed with clothes that are too small, and the toy box doesn't overflow. More importantly, our children have been taught the joy of giving. Sometimes we think of specific person who can use or enjoy the item we are giving away. Other times we give it to a local charity thrift store. The important part of the process is teaching joy of giving. Plus our children have learned that possessions aren't to be horded.

Involve your preschooler in charitable activities to learn to give of self. My children, and now my grandchildren, go with me when I serve meals-on-wheels. When they ask why we do it, I tell them it is because other people need us to.

Your child doesn't need a reward or payment for every act of kindness. Our children should learn to love, help, share, and give for its own sake. The prize is seeing someone else happy and the sense of satisfaction, which comes from their actions.

These are all trait that are best learned at home––where love begins––not in a preschool with twenty or thirty other selfish little beings all vying for a small amount of love and attention from a caregiver.

As children learn self-discipline and practice these character qualities they begin to learn social skills. This must begin at home and not wait until you are away from home where certain manners and decorum are expected.

Manners

As soon as a child begins talking, learning to say "please," "thank you," "hello," "good-bye" can begin. By the age of three most children can speak quietly, not to interrupt, and greet other people. Maria Montessori says three-year-olds can learn to shake hands, sit in a restaurant, and ask permission to leave the room.

Inge Canon states that a firm foundation of etiquette can be laid before a child is three. Her suggestions include eye contact when someone is speaking, not whining, picking up toys, coming immediately when called, and knowing the limits of the word "no." And those limits will include when the child may or may not use that word.

My daughter remarked that often people comment about the fact that when she finishes a meal in another person's home, she clears her eating-place. So few people do that. My daughter learned this kindness as a child.

By teaching children to talk nicely to others, including siblings and animals, from the very beginning of speech, children will develop an other-focused attitude. We often hear tales of children embarrassing their parents or others with inappropriate conversation, and it is thought of as cute. Children can be taught early that some topics are not appropriate to talk about.

Three- and four-year-olds are always on the move. They can, however, learn to move quietly indoors, not run in buildings, not to let doors slam, and watch out for older people.

It is also normal for a preschooler to be wiggly and have a short attention span. It's abnormal for these little ones to sit for a lengthy time at a table to do "schoolwork." But, like movement, children can learn to sit quietly when appropriate. Again learning to sit quietly is best taught at home before going out.

Teach at Home

Many at-home situations provide opportunities to teach quiet sitting and walking. As soon as your baby is sitting in a high chair, teach being quiet at the table. Don't allow banging utensils or screaming, no matter how cute. Stop food throwing as soon as it begins.

Children can learn to sit quietly by sitting during a read aloud time or watching a video. You can even help your toddler and preschooler sit quietly while visiting with company. Begin with your child sitting on your lap. As quieting sitting is learned, your child can sit next to you, and later in another chair.

Don't push your child beyond the limits of tolerance. Start with a minute or two, then build from there. When you are in a public setting, don't be embarrassed to remove an unruly child. Yes, you may miss a few minutes of the sermon or conversation. But you will be giving your child future benefits that cannot be measured by a little inconvenience now.

When my son was eight years old, we went to a full production of Handel's *Messiah*. As you may know it is a very long, and not very visual, performance. During intermission, he was asked how he was enjoying it. After he responded, this mother told me that she was amazed that he was able to sit through such a program, and enjoy it. My son had been taught from babyhood.

This is a hefty amount of learning and teaching. If you are spending time teaching all of these things, there is little time for sit-down academics. However children who learn early to respect other people and have self-discipline are ready to learn. A youngster who is able to listen, follow directions and rules, sit quietly, and work carefully will be able to make the most of learning time later on.

One evening we had a guest in for dinner. Our four-year-old granddaughter reached for his hand to pray before the meal, as is our custom. She said her small prayer, put her napkin on her lap, and ate her meal quietly while the adults had conversation. When she was finished eating, she asked to be excused.

Our guest was delighted to see her thoughtful behavior, which seems to come naturally. My granddaughter's manners didn't come naturally. She learned them with careful and consistent instruction at each meal we have.

Teaching self-control, character qualities, and social skills is hard work for parent and child. If you are consistently teaching these qualities, you are teaching a full curriculum. The benefits as your child grows up are innumerable. You are laying a foundation now, which will serve your child well throughout life.

References

1. Benedict, Mark, "The Importance of Discipling Early," Christian Parents.net, http://www.christian-parents.net/Children/C107_Early_Discipline.htm (accessed August 2009, site now discontinued).
2. The Center for Character Development, "Core Ethical Values," Lubbock Christian University, http://www.CharacterCenter.com/CoreEthicalValues.html.

Web Resources

Better Than Preschool
www.betterthanpreschool.com

Exploring Homeschooling
"Why Not to Put Your Child in Preschool"
www.exploringhomeschooling.com/ReasonsWhyNOTtoPutYourC
hildinPreschool.aspx

Universal Preschool
www.universalpreschool.com

Child Fun
www.childfun.com

Starfall
www.starfall.com

PBS Parents
www.pbs.org/parents

Literacy Center Education Network
www.literacycenter.net

Preschool Express
www.preschoolexpress.com>
First School Preschool Activities
www.first-school.ws/index.htm

DLTK's Sites
www.dltk-kids.com

Ed Helper
www.edhelper.com

Preschool Education
www.preschooleducation.com

Dollar Stretchers
"Twenty Toys You Don't Have to Buy"
by Colleen Moulding

www.stretcher.com/stories/00/000221c.cfm

Songs and Poems to Learn Shoe Tying
www.atozkidsstuff.com/shoes.html

Kiddie Records
Recordings of records from the 1950s and 60s
www.kiddierecords.com

A to Z Kid Stuff
www.atozkidsstuff.com

Make Stuff
www.make-stuff.com/kids

AHC Arts & Crafts
Helping Kids with Art
www.artistshelpingchildren.org

Ivy Joy
PDF coloring books
www.ivyjoy.com/coloring/pdflinks.html

100 Picture Books Everyone Should Know
http://kids.nypl.org/reading/recommended2.cfm?ListID=61

Letter of the Week
www.letteroftheweek.com

Child Care Lounge
Preschool Science Fun and Experiments
www.childcarelounge.com/activity/science-experiments.php

Science for Preschoolers
http://scienceforpreschoolers.com
Science Intro
www.kids.scintro.com

Outdoor Fun Store
Free Fun Stuff
www.outdoorfunstore.com/freefun.asp

Print Resources

I have purposely excluded curriculum from this list. The resources listed will help you understand that formal academics aren't needed to help your young child have a good foundation for later educational pursuit.

Ames, Louise Bates, Your Two-Year-Old: Terrible or Tender, Dell, 1983.

_____, Your Four-Year-Old: Wild and Wonderful, Dell, 1989.

_____, Your Five-Year-Old: Sunny and Serene, Dell, 1981.

_____ and Ilg, Francis, Your Three-Year-Old: Friend or Enemy, Dell, 1980.

Bruer, John T., The Myth of the First Three Years: A New Understanding of Early Brain Development, The Free Press, 1999.

Crain, William C., Reclaiming Childhood, Letting Children Be Children in Our Achievement-Oriented Society, Henry Holt & Co., 2003.

Elkind, David, Miseducation: Preschoolers at Risk, Knopf, 1997.

_____, The Hurried Child, De Capo Press, Twenty-fifth Anniversary, 2006.

_____, The Power of Play: Learning What Comes Naturally, De Capo Press, 2007.

Hymowitz, Kay S., Ready or Not: why treating children as small adults endangers their future—and ours, Simon & Shuster, 1999.

Kirp, David L., The Sandbox Investment: the preschool movement and kids-first politics, Harvard Press, 2007.

Moore, Raymond & Dorothy, Better Late Than Early: A New Approach to Your Child's Education, Reader's Digest Association, 1989.

_____, School Can Wait, Hewitt Research Foundation, 1989.

_____, Home Grown Kids: A Practical Handbook for Teaching Your Children at Home, The Moore Foundation, 1981.

Olfman, Shama, All Work and No Play ...:How Educational Reforms Are Harming Our Preschoolers, Greenwood Publishing Group, 2003.

Paley, Vivian Gussin, A Child's Work: The Importance of Fantasy Play, University of Chicago Press, 2007.